Advantages of Moving into a 55+ Park

Advantages of Moving into a 55+ Park

How to Enjoy Your Retirement Even on a Budget

Jerry Minchey

Stony River Media

Minchey, Jerry. Advantages of Moving into a 55+ Park: how
to enjoy your retirement, even on a budget / Jerry Minchey

ISBN 10: 0-9844968-2-3
ISBN 13: 978-0-9844968-2-2

1. Retirement communities.
2. Retirement, Places of.
3. Retirement.

Published by Stony River Media
Asheville, North Carolina
StonyRiverMedia.com

I am indebted to Marilyn Minchey, Patricia Benton, Corrine Canace, and Brent Minchey without whose help and suggestions this book would not exist.

Don't simply retire *from* something; have something to retire *to*.

~ *Rev. Harry Emerson Fosdick*

Contents

Introduction

Many people, as they approach retirement, look forward to living in an active 55+ community. They look forward to the variety of activities going on, the kid-free and motorcycle-free environment, and not having to worry about maintenance, yard work, and other homeowner chores.

They also have a lot of questions and there's a lot they want to know about the cost and what's involved in this lifestyle.

The purpose of this book is to answer those questions, and if you're among those wondering, to help you decide if it's the right lifestyle for you and to look at a few other options. Let's start with some terminology.

Mobile & Manufactured Homes & Trailer Parks

We've all heard the terms "55+ mobile home park" and "trailer park." Those terms are still commonly used even though the industry officially changed to "community" or "manufactured homes" in 1978.

Some of the homes can be moved on a truck, but they are not really very mobile. Most of them have patios, screened-in porches, etc. and are more or less permanent.

It's like the phrase, unleaded gas. All gasoline is now unleaded. Leaded gas could no longer be sold in the US as of December 31st, 1995, but the phrase "unleaded gas" is still in common use (implying that you have the option of buying leaded gas – which you don't). It looks like it takes a generation or more for the use of a term to die out.

Anyway, "mobile home park" and "trailer park" are still in common use and you still see them on signs in front of some parks, but in this book I will use the 'new' phrases—manufactured home parks, or communities, or just parks.

55+ Communities

The next thing to define is the type of 55+ community most of this book will be referring to. Some 55+ communities or "active adult communities," as they are sometimes called, are in high-rise condo buildings and some communities have 3,000 to 5,000 square-foot, stand-alone homes that sell for a million dollars or more.

Some are in gated communities that have restaurants and shops within the gates. Even though a lot of the comments and advice in this book would be helpful when deciding to move into one of these communities, this book is more involved with retiring on a much lower budget.

I will mainly be talking about manufactured homes in the $5,000 to $50,000 range. Yes, you can find nice (but small) homes in the $5,000 to $10,000 range, but the typical manufactured homes you'll find will likely be in the $20,000 to $30,000 range. I will talk more about home prices and what's available in a later chapter.

Living in a 55+ community, or park, may be ideal for you or it may not. In this book I'm going to arm you with the facts, give you the pros and cons, and include some inside information so you don't have to learn everything the hard way. Making your decision to move into a 55+ community (and which one) gets easier the more information you have access to.

That's the purpose of this book. I want to give you a lot of information and outline the questions to ask so you can get even more information. Consider your decision-making process and your selection process an adventure and enjoy the journey.

Let's get started.

Chapter 1

What Is It Like to Live in a 55+ Park?

Of course, the best way to find out what it's like to live in a 55+ park would be to actually live in one for a while. The second best way would be to talk to people who are currently living in one of the parks or who have lived in one.

Visiting a park and talking to some of the residents is another good way to learn even more about the lifestyle, but this book will arm you with even more information and help you get the most out of your visits.

Later in your decision-making process it will be important for you to visit the actual park you are considering moving into. 55+ parks vary. How big they are, how old they are, and the makeup and interests of the people living there all go into defining the culture of the park.

With all of that said, let me give you some firsthand examples of life in different parks that I'm familiar with.

My cousin lived in a park for 15 years. He knew almost everyone in the park. This park bordered a lake and many people in the park had small power boats. He didn't do a lot of fishing, but he loved to go out in his boat and just relax. There were creeks and canals he could explore and, when he had out-of-town guests, he would always take them out for a boat ride. The little boat didn't go much faster than a rowboat, but he wasn't in a hurry, so it didn't matter.

My mother and father lived in a different park. What my father liked best was playing shuffleboard. Most afternoons, if he wasn't up from his nap by the time the shuffleboard games started, someone would knock on the door and ask my mother: "Can Charles come out and play? We need one more for shuffleboard."

Most people spend a lot of time outside walking, sitting on their screened-in porch, playing games, working in their flower gardens, or sitting by the pool. In the process of being out and about all of the time, they see and visit with almost everyone in the park.

One woman told me, "My life is no longer controlled by what's on TV."

Park Cultures

Each park is different. In some parks I see a lot of people walking and stopping to talk with each other. In another park it seems like almost everyone has what they call tricycles (Those are bikes with two wheels on the back so people can go as slow as they want to and not have to worry about maintaining their balance).

I don't know why these have become popular in one park and not so much so in others. As I said, the culture in each park is different.

One man has a small building right behind his home. He calls it his woodworking shop. It isn't very big at all. In fact, there is only room for him to stand inside the shop. When anyone stops to talk to him, they have to stay outside by the open door.

He has more woodworking tools in his shop than I have ever seen even in a big shop. He doesn't make furniture or big items. He makes little items that fit in your hand. I don't think he sells many (if any) items because he is always giving his work away.

My mother asked him to make her four little wooden trays to hold Scrabble pieces so the pieces would stand up and be easy to see. He made the four pieces and each one was made out of a different kind of wood.

They were beautiful, but he wouldn't let her pay him. I could go on with such stories, but I think you get the general idea of what life is like in a 55+ park.

Your Neighbors

One of the things I find most interesting is the backgrounds of the people in the parks. It seems that most of them have had very interesting lives.

One woman I know sang with the NY Philharmonic Orchestra; one man spent his life as a photographer for the National Geographic magazine.

Of course, not everyone has led what I consider interesting lives. I know a man who has spent all of his life working in a GM factory. He didn't like his job, but didn't see any way out of it. He couldn't leave and get a job that paid him nearly as much as he was making. He lived his whole life looking forward to retirement. Now that he is retired, he is having the time of his life and seems to enjoy retirement more than anyone else. He is one of the friendliest people in the park.

I had two cousins who lived next door to each other in Ohio. One had a home in a 55+ park and spent every winter there for many years. He kept trying to persuade his brother to get a winter home there and join him, but his brother wasn't interested. He would say, "Why would I want to go to Florida and sit in a little tin box all winter?"

Then one time he came down for a visit. After a week and a half, he went back home to Ohio. He told one of his friends, "You know, they do more down there in a week than I do here all winter."

How Park Life Is Different

Probably the biggest difference between the 55+ park lifestyle and the residents' previous lifestyles can be broken down into four areas:

You will be more active

There are always things to do: games to play, social get-togethers, and things to keep you mentally and physically active and alert. Of course, it's like the remote control for your TV—you are in charge. You can turn the TV (or the world) off when you want to and you can change channels when you want to. You will find the 55+ park kind of like cable TV with over 100 channels. You can always find something you like.

You will be more socially involved

You will know practically all of your neighbors—and probably everyone in the park. Everyone who passes by will speak to you, ask about your grandkids, and really be interested in you. You will find activities such as a Thursday morning breakfast at a different restaurant every week; there's the Friday night fish fry at a restaurant on the lake and the Tuesday night pizza party. Of course, you probably won't go to all of these weekly events—at least not every week. That's one of the interesting things about the events: you never know who you are going to see.

You will be more relaxed and have less stress
Even when there are serious health problems to deal with, it seems that these people are not stressed out. They always seem upbeat and happy. Maybe it's because people who are stressed out or negative don't choose the 55+ park life. Maybe just being out in the fresh air and getting some exercise walking around takes the stress away, but, for whatever reason, one thing is for sure—you won't find much stress in a 55+ park.

You will be around happy people with positive attitudes
I don't like to be around negative people or people who never do anything or don't get around to making decisions. You won't find these people in 55+ parks. For one thing, they wouldn't be there if they had not made a decision. It's like the old saying, "Some people make things happen, some people watch things happen, and some people wonder what happened." In a 55+ park, you will find mostly people who make things happen. You won't find many in the "wonder what happened" group.

You're Not Locked In

One other good thing about living in a 55+ community is that it's easy to change your mind. If you find that you don't like the lifestyle, or you decide you want to live somewhere else, you can usually sell your home in a matter of weeks—maybe even days.

Twice my parents sold their home in a 55+ park in a matter of days—and made a profit both times.

Moving is usually easy too. The customs are different for different parts of the country, but in many parks it's normal to sell a home in a 55+ community with everything included in the purchase price. That includes dishes, dish towels, bath towels, sheets, silverware, etc. In other words, pack your suitcase and toothbrush and walk out. That's not always the way it's done, but often it is.

Selling a home in a 55+ community is not like selling a brick and stick house where it could take months or even years to sell. It's more like selling a car. You can do it in a hurry.

Finding Out If It's Right for You

Now you have a little insight into the lifestyle you can expect. You won't see all of this if you just drive around or walk around a park. You can learn a lot and get a feel for what life would be like if you walk around and talk to people, but it takes time to really understand and appreciate the different lifestyle you will experience living in a 55+ park.

If this sounds interesting to you, do some more investigating by reading the rest of this book, thinking about which area you would like to live in, visit some parks, and most importantly, make a decision.

You may decide that this is not the lifestyle for you, and it's not right for everyone, but at least make a decision. Don't let the reason you didn't move into a 55+ park be because you just never got around to making a decision.

One way to dip your toe in the water, so to speak, is to buy or rent a small place and spend a winter in one of these parks. That will give you some firsthand knowledge and experience to help you make your decision.

Chapter 2

Where Is the Best Place to Retire?

A recent article in Money magazine had a list of the ten best places to retire and their list might surprise you. Here is a link to the article and more like it:

BestOf55Plus.com/retirelinks

I disagree with their list. In fact, I wouldn't want to retire to any of the 10 places they named.

Many magazines and websites come out with lists of best places to retire all the time. It's an easy article to write and it always gets attention.

The main reason I disagree with these lists is that the criteria they used to select the places on their list are not things that are very important to me—at least, not now.

For example, low taxes and access to good healthcare are high on most lists.

Property tax, sales tax, and income tax are not as important to me as they were earlier in life when I was making more money and owned higher-priced property.

Think about your own situation. After you retire you probably will not own a lot of real property (maybe none if you're renting) and your taxable income will probably be lower.

Finally, sales tax is not as important as it once was because you probably won't be buying a lot of taxable items, like new lawn mowers, big screen TVs, etc. (I did buy a big screen TV recently, but I bought it online and there was no sales tax.)

Even your food costs will be a lot less than they were when you were working and maybe had a house full of kids, so sales tax on food (if there is any) and other items would not be really important—at least it's not for me. In other words, it isn't a big enough factor for it to be something that I would consider when deciding where I would choose to live.

Also, good health care is available almost everywhere.

The things that are important to me are climate, being reasonably close to family and friends (at least, part of the year), and being in a place where the music and culture are the type I like.

For example, if you like fishing, you won't find a lot of places to fish in Arizona or West Texas; if you like Cajun music, you probably won't find much of that in Kansas. I like old time mountain music, but it's not big in Arizona. Find out if the activities you enjoy are popular in the locations you're considering.

Climate

I think climate is important to most people. That's why so many people retire to Florida or Arizona. You don't see many people retiring to New York or Minnesota. I have some friends who live in New York in the summer and Hilton Head Island, South Carolina, in the winter.

Climate is relative. I have friends who live in Tampa, FL, in the summer, but go to Ft. Myers, FL, in the winter because Tampa gets "so cold." I know people who live in Connecticut in the winter, but go to Maine in the summer because Connecticut gets "so hot."

I have friends who live in Iowa in the summer and in Asheville, North Carolina, in the winter because Asheville is so much warmer. Of course, I have friends who live in Asheville in the summer and go to Florida in the winter because they think Asheville gets too cold in the winter.

In other words, what is hot and what is cold is subjective and relative to what you're used to.

Bottom line, look for a place where you will have access to the lifestyle you like, the climate you like, and where you are reasonably close to family and friends (if that's important to you). Of course, none of these things may be important to you, so think about what is.

Family, Friends, and Other Connections

One other thing to consider is that a lot of people don't want to move away from the family and friends. Many people like to live near the same area where they have lived for years. There are a lot of advantages to that—their friends are there, more than likely a lot of relatives (maybe even grandkids) are nearby, and they are familiar with the area. They know where everything is and know who to trust to do repair work.

Another factor to consider is that the doctors they know and trust are in the area.

Warmer is Not for Everyone

So retiring and moving off to a warmer climate is not for everyone. There are 55+ parks in every state and, if you're inside most of the time, whether it's hot or cold outside the weather may not be as big of a concern as it used to be for you. In fact, snow is pretty if you get to sit inside and enjoy it. Not having to get out in the snow and go to work changes your attitude about it.

One thing a lot of people tell me that they miss about not living where they used to live is the four seasons. They miss the beautiful colors in the fall, the first snowfall of the year, and the refreshing green trees and flowers in the spring.

Of course, you can't have everything—unless you choose to live in two places. We'll talk about that in a later chapter. It's not as expensive as you would think and a lot of people enjoy that lifestyle.

Chapter 3

How Much Will It Cost?

The first thing everyone wants to know when considering whether to move into a 55+ community is how much it will cost.

The real answer is that it's within your budget. How do I know that? Because it's within almost anyone's budget. Since you've bought this book and are considering it, you can afford it.

Ask Yourself the Right Question

Most people go about thinking about being able to afford retirement backwards. They wonder, How much money do I need for retirement? Look at it the other way. Here's how much money I have; what kind of retirement can I afford and sustain with this amount of money and income?

People ask, "Should I retire or keep working?" The answer is simple. Consider the life you have now. How much do you like it or hate it? Compare that to the life you would have if you were to retire now.

If you want to keep your same 4-bedroom brick house with two new cars in the driveway and belong to the same country club, maybe you need to keep working. A lot of people enjoy that life and want to hold on to it as long as possible.

But if you're ready for something different, let's look at some options. First of all, living in a 55+ community is not necessarily better or worse than how you're living now, it's just different. It's a lifestyle many people love, but it's not for everyone.

You will have less income if you retire now than you would if you keep working, but which lifestyle will make you happier?

These are decisions that only you can make. For many people work is their life. They are good at what they do and people look up to them; they feel important on the job; it gives them a purpose in life and they actually enjoy working—sometimes way more than they think.

Other people hate every minute at work.

What Can You Afford?

You're on this earth and you have to live somewhere. Living in a 55+ community is one of the most inexpensive options you'll find. Of course, there are some very nice 55+ parks where you can spend a fortune and live in the utmost luxury.

It's like buying a car. You can buy a car for less than $3,000 to over $300,000. You can do the same with a home in a 55+ community.

Sit down and add up your retirement income. How much will be coming in each month from Social Security? How much from any pension or investments you have? How much cash (or things that can be converted into cash) do you have—your home, your investments, etc.?

With this information you can decide what kind of retirement house you can afford. In almost every case, it will come down to deciding which home to live in (buy or rent) and not whether to do it.

Whether you choose to live in a 55+ community full-time or part-time, one thing is for sure—you will find that it's a different lifestyle from the one you're used to.

Let's get on to talking about what this chapter is really about—the cost of homes and the fees involved when living in a 55+ community.

Why Cheap Can Be Upscale

But before we do that, there's one more thing I want to point out. I don't want to get into trouble by generalizing or not being politically correct, but when you think about living in a low-priced home, you think about it being in a bad or undesirable neighborhood and maybe living near crime and riff-raff in general.

That's not the case in 55+ parks. You will find people living in a $10,000 retirement home who have a half-million dollar home somewhere else.

All of your life it seems that everyone strives to live in the biggest house they can afford (or maybe a little bigger) and have the nicest cars, etc. People work hard in the rat race to achieve this lifestyle and some aren't able to switch gears to enjoy retirement.

But in 55+ parks your neighbors are the people who decided that life is no longer about things. They're the people who make an active decision to make their retirement about activities, friends, having fun, no stress, and, enjoying life in general. It turns out you don't need a big fancy house for that.

Now I will get off of my soapbox and get down to the cost of homes and the fees involved.

Fees

First of all, it's not just the cost of the home you have to consider. Unlike living in a traditional subdivision, in a 55+ community, there are fees that can get substantial. These fees go by different names and I will describe them in more detail later in the chapter. For now, just know that they are a major expense to be considered.

For example, you can find fairly nice homes on the market for $5,000, but sometimes the catch is that they are locked into high monthly fees. Usually the fees are reasonable for what you get.

One of my proofreaders circled the $5,000 number above and said, "Really?" I sent her a link to the listings on BestOf55Plus.com where she found four homes for sale in one area that were priced from $3,000 to $5,000 (and that was the asking price). These homes were listed on Craigslist.

Here are some examples:

A friend just bought a three bedroom home on a golf course in a 55+ community for $35,000. The monthly fees are $650 and that is a little high, but it's a very nice park. You get what you pay for.

The monthly HOA (Home Owner Association) fees range from less than $200 a month to over $1,000, but $300 to $400 a month is a typical mid-range. Of course, it all depends on what's included.

Be sure to check out the fees carefully on any home you're considering. Also check to see if there have been any assessments. Some parks have low monthly fees but then have assessments every time money is needed for something. Other parks have higher fees and keep a reserve fund for major or unexpected expenses.

The Rules

Of course, look closely at the rules or bylaws. By all means, get a copy of the rules and read them carefully. Don't depend on statements made by the seller or the agent.

You don't want to move in and then find out that you can't keep your boat in your driveway or that your grandkids can only stay two weeks a year and only two at a time max. Of course, if you don't own a boat or don't have grandkids, you might like this rule.

Many parks have a rule that you can't rent your home out, it has to be occupied by the owner. This is generally a good rule and most people like it.

Just don't look at your new home as an investment thinking that, if you don't like it, you can just rent it out. If that's a thought in the back of your mind, check the rules and make sure that this is permitted before you buy your home.

Be careful if someone says, "Yea, that's in the rules, but they don't enforce that."

Other Costs

Also, know what your property taxes and insurance costs will be. Just because the son of the owner says, "I think the taxes run about $500 a year," don't depend on that. See it in writing. Check with the county tax office.

Insurance is another factor to consider. There are several factors that make insurance rates vary all over the place. How old the home is makes a difference. Laws have changed to make newer manufactured homes much better at withstanding hurricanes and tornadoes. Insurance rates will be higher on older homes.

Also, which area you're in will make a difference. What is the likelihood of a flood, tornado or hurricane where your home is located? Even a few miles one way or the other can make a big difference in your insurance rate.

Getting Current Prices

One way to get an idea of what homes are selling for in different areas is to search eBay and Craigslist.

When you're searching either of these websites, search for each of the following keywords:

- Mobile home

- Manufactured home

- Double wide home

- Trailer

- Modular home

- 55+

You will need to search using each of these terms in order to see all of the listings because, unfortunately, there is not one single term that is universally used to describe the retirement homes in a 55+ park.

As I said earlier in the book, the homes are not really mobile and they are not trailers now and most of them never were, but the above terms are still in common use by the people who will be posting the listings.

The correct term is, 'manufactured home' (as of 1978), but, for now, it is probably the least used term. It will catch on in due time.

Bottom line: To find typical prices on homes in 55+ parks, check out eBay and Craigslist listings on BestOf55Plus.com. This will give you an idea of the market prices. Then go visit the areas and check out the different 55+ parks and talk with some owners and agents.

The more you investigate, the less you have to invest

Keep in mind that most of the asking prices for 55+ homes are very negotiable. It's a common situation where a parent died or moved into a nursing home and the kids called an agent and told them to sell the place. They don't know what it's worth; they just want it sold so they are not sitting there paying the monthly HOA fees. They're not likely to turn down a reasonable offer. In fact, you may find that they won't turn down an unreasonable offer.

Some people don't like to negotiate, but in the 55+ home market almost all prices are negotiable. You can save a lot of money by doing just a little bit of negotiating. Use the simple negotiating techniques described below and you will save a lot of money.

My 7 All-Time Favorite Negotiating Phrases for People Who Don't Like to Negotiate

Notice that in none of these phrases are you actually saying that you won't pay the amount the person is asking, so you can always accept the proposal and go forward with the purchase.

#1 ALWAYS, ALWAYS flinch at the first price or proposal

You should almost fall out of your chair because you are so shocked. Do this even if the price you hear is way less than what you expected. Flinch and say, "That's WAY out of my budget," and then shut up. Don't say a word. Just sit and wait for the price to drop.

#2. Next, when you get the lower price quote, you should say, "You've got to do better that that."

And then, again, you shut up. If you open your mouth, you won't get the next price concession. If you say yes to the first offer, the other person will know that they quoted you a price that was too low. They may even try to find a way to increase the price. They may say something like, "Well let me see if the boss will go along with this price" or, "Let me make sure that this is ok with my wife."

#3. If you make a counter offer, ALWAYS ask for a much lower price than you expect to get

One of the cardinal rules of negotiating is that you should ask the other side for more than you expect to get. Henry Kissinger went so far as to say, "Effectiveness at the negotiating table depends upon overstating one's demands."

#4. Never offer to split the difference

It's human nature to want to 'play fair'. Our sense of fair play dictates to us that, if both sides give equally, then that's fair. The other side is almost always willing to split the difference, so you should try to get a little better deal than that.

#5. Use two powerful negotiating techniques all in one sentence. The two techniques are: "If I could, would you?" and 'absent higher authority'

We've all experienced the 'absent higher authority' technique. For example, "Our insurance regulations won't let you go back in the shop," or "The loan committee wouldn't go along with those terms."

You don't get to talk to the loan committee (it doesn't exist) and you don't get to talk to the insurance company. It's a higher authority that you can't talk to.

Here's how to use it in your favor for once.

When you're down to the final negotiations, you can say, "If I could get my (financial adviser, spouse, or some absent higher authority) to go along with this, would you replace the carpet in the living room?"

Notice that, in this statement, you haven't agreed to anything.

The owner or salesperson is in a position of feeling that he/she needs to go along with what you're proposing to keep the deal from falling apart.

#6. Nibble for more at the end

You can usually get a little bit more even after you have basically agreed on everything—if you will use a technique I call nibbling.

You can say, "You ARE going to have the carpets professionally cleaned," or "You are going to replace the kitchen faucet, aren't you?"

The sales person is already thinking about what she is going to do with her commission. The last thing she wants is for this sale to fall through. She will usually give just a little more if you 'nibble'.

#7. When you're getting close to the end of the negotiations and everything is just about nailed down, say, "I'm getting nervous about this" and then SHUT UP

The other party will think the deal is about to fall apart and they will likely throw in one more concession to seal the deal.

Bottom line: Use some or all of the above negotiating techniques and you can easily cut the price you end up paying for your new home by thousands of dollars.

Chapter 4

How to Find the Best Parks

The first step in finding the 'perfect' park for you is to think about where in the country you want to live. Now, maybe for the first time in your life, you get to decide where you want to live.

For most of your life you have had to live where you had a job. Of course, sometimes you had a little choice—you got a job offer in Dallas, Phoenix and Atlanta and you had to make a choice. But now you can choose almost any state and city anywhere, maybe even in another country. I'll discuss that in a later chapter.

What Part of the Country?

First, narrow down the possibilities. This is usually pretty easy—you decide that you don't want to live where there are harsh winters, you've had enough of shoveling snow, etc.

If you decide that you want to live in an area that's warm all the time, that eliminates about 80% of the US, but you still have to decide whether you like Florida, Arizona, Southern California or one of several other areas that are always warm.

I love visiting the West – Arizona, New Mexico, Colorado, etc. – but I couldn't live there. I'm used to high humidity and the dry air is hard on my nose and skin. Maybe I would get used to it.

On the other hand, I have friends from the Southwest and they start complaining about the high humidity as soon as they get off the plane when they come to visit me. This was especially true when I lived on Hilton Head Island, South Carolina.

Here's another weather concern. I had a friend who moved from Florida to Whidbey Island off the coast of Washington state. He had visited there and loved it. After living there for six months, he moved back to Florida. He said that he almost never saw the sun the whole six months he was there. He said that he took sunshine for granted just like oxygen. He said that he needed the sunshine to be happy.

Bottom line: put some thought into the general area where you would like to live first. Of course, you may have already decided that years ago.

Choose a City

After you have decided on a general area, you're ready to get down to seriously selecting a city to be in (or near).

For example, if you have decided that you want to move to Florida, that's a big state and you still have a lot to consider. Do you want to be near the beach or do you want to be inland? If you want to be near the ocean, there's a world of difference between the Atlantic side and the Gulf side. Most people living near the ocean in Florida would not want to move to the opposite coast. There are pros and cons to each. Do you want to be in southern Florida, where it's a lot warmer during the winter (and hotter in summer)?

Of course, there are a lot of other things to consider in addition to the weather. What activities do you like to do? How close do you want to be to family and friends? How close do you want to be to your grandkids? Of course, they may be scattered all over the country. If you're going to be flying to see them from time to time, instead of driving, there is not a lot of difference in time or cost to fly most places.

Friends and Relatives

Another thing to consider when selecting where you want to live is do you have any friends or relatives already living in a 55+ park? I know of one 55+ park where about a fourth of the park is made up of people from the same city in Michigan. They keep telling their friends about how nice the area is and how much they enjoy it and, as their friends retire, many of them move into the same park. In another park about 10% of the people are related.

People who are living in a 55+ park know who's not coming back next year or who has died and they know which homes are available at a very good price and they tell their friends and relatives.

Even if you don't necessarily want to live in a park where a lot of your friends or relatives live, it's a good idea to talk to them. Find out what they like and dislike about the lifestyle and the area. They have a wealth of information. Some of it may be biased, of course, but hear what they have to say.

Visit First

After you have narrowed your search down to a few areas, you can't beat actually going to visit them. Some parks have homes to rent. Renting before you buy is a good way to see if you like the area. And since many homes are sold completely furnished, and I mean completely—right down to dish towels and sheets—moving in is no big deal. Just bring your toothbrush.

My cousin rented a home for a week before he bought his home which was in the same park. Of course, if you can rent the exact home you are considering buying, that would really help you make up your mind. Even staying in a motel for a week or two will give you a feel of the neighborhood and allow you to check out several parks in the surrounding area.

When You are Ready to Buy

When you decide on a general area you want to live in, be sure to check craigslist.org and eBay. I prefer craigslist for finding homes, but be sure to check them both out.

On craigslist and eBay you can see pictures and prices. Of course, there is usually a difference between the asking price and the selling price. Sometimes a big difference.

If you search eBay for "Sold" items, you can see what a home actually sold for. That's a lot better information than just seeing what someone is asking for a home.

Keep in mind that, in Florida and a lot of other states, buying a home in a 55+ park is more like buying a car than it is like buying a home. You will get a title with a VIN (vehicle identification number) instead of a deed.

When you get down to making a written offer (or at least, when you get ready to close the deal), I would recommend that you consult with an attorney. There is not much to the transaction so an attorney won't charge you much. Keep in mind that, in some cases, you may be buying a share of the park, so there could be a little more involved. That's another reason that I would recommend that you consult an attorney.

Remember, the more you investigate the less you have to invest. There are a lot of good deals in 55+ parks. Take your time and find one.

One of the major reasons there are so many good deals is that there is a constant turnover. When someone dies or moves into an assisted living home, their home in the 55+ park goes on the market.

Often, owners will buy another (maybe higher priced) home in the same park when it becomes available and then sell their existing home. The result is the same—another house goes on the market.

You could search forever to find the perfect deal. Don't go that route. Do a reasonable amount of research, find a home and a price that you like, make a deal and move in. You can always sell it and buy another home later.

One other thing to consider is that some parks have a high percentage of snowbirds living there. In other words, a lot of the residents are only there during the winter months and the park could be a lot less occupied during the summer months. Some people like the quiet season and some find it too dull. If this is of concern to you, be sure to check it out before buying.

One last point, be sure to check all of the things listed in the Buyer Checklist chapter. By all means, read over the rules and regulations carefully before you buy a home.

Most of the rules are reasonable and include the restrictions you would want, but sometimes ridiculous rules get included. I know of one park that had a rule that you can have a maximum of six goldfish. Do they think the goldfish will make too much noise? To me that's more comical than being a restriction that anyone would pay attention to.

Chapter 5

Co-ops, Rental Parks, and Owner-Occupied Lots

I'm not a lawyer and the information in this chapter is not legal advice. In fact, as I've said before, nothing in this book is to be considered to be legal advice. I just wanted to say it again here to make sure that point is absolutely understood.

This is my understanding of the definitions and descriptions of some of the terms described. I have tried to put the information in layman's terms. Consult an attorney for legal advice and for exact and detailed information.

Co-op

A Co-op is short for cooperative housing corporation. In a 55+ park the Co-op usually owns the land, utilities and community facilities (clubhouse, etc). You would own a share (sometimes called a membership) in the cooperative housing corporation.

As part of your membership in the co-op, you have an exclusive right to live in a specified unit for as long as you pay your fees and abide by the rules.

You also get to vote in the business of the corporation just like a shareholder in any other corporation.

There could be a minor tax advantage to being in a co-op. You will be able to deduct your share of the taxes and the interest paid on the mortgage (if there is one), but you have no personal liability for paying off the mortgage.

Owner Occupied

"Owner occupied" or "resident owned" (as it's sometimes called) means that you don't pay rent for a lot. You pay a maintenance fee which is usually much less.

It also means that you are a shareholder and own a share of the community. You do not actually own the individual lot that your home is sitting on.

Rental Park

A rental park (as the name implies) means that you don't own anything. You are simply renting or leasing the lot that your home is on. You could be renting the actual home also.

Renting doesn't tie up much of your capital and, if you decide the 55+ park lifestyle is not for you (or if you decide you want to live in a different place), it's easy to move.

You will probably be obligated until the end of the lease, but usually there is a waiting list and you can get someone to take over your lease in very short order.

My experience is that you can sell a home in the 55+ park very quickly—usually in a matter of a few weeks to a month or two at the most. Of course, there's no guarantee that you can sell that quickly. It's like selling car. How long would it take you to sell your car if you decided to?

Summary

As was stated at the beginning of this chapter, this is a short, layman's overview of the different 55+ park arrangements. This information is intended to give you a working knowledge of the basic differences and is not intended to cover all aspects of the topic.

You can get more information from your agent (if you're going through an agent) or from a lawyer who specializes in this field.

Don't make it over complicated. In my opinion, it's not a big deal. Finding the area of the country where you want to live and then finding a park and then a home you like is much more important.

Chapter 6

How Much Do Homes in a 55+ Park Cost?

Home prices in 55+ parks are all over the place. You can find homes ranging from $5,000 to well over a million—not in the same park of course.

One big difference between living in a home in a 55+ park and living in a typical neighborhood is that, in a typical neighborhood, most people buy a house that's as expensive as they can afford (or sometimes a little more expensive than they can afford). That's not the case in a 55+ park.

I know of a case where a couple had over half a million dollars in the bank and they were living in a $5,000 home in a 55+ park.

Many people decide that, when they retire, they don't need or want a big expensive house. It's not a status symbol like it was when they were in the rat race. They don't want a big house to clean. They don't have a lot of company and they find that they are happier with a smaller (and less expensive) house.

I know plenty of people in 55+ parks living in $20,000 to $30,000 homes (with three bedrooms and two baths) and the homes are very nice.

One big difference you will find in 55+ parks is that, when you're living in a low-price home, you are not living next to riff-raff like you possibly would in a conventional neighborhood.

A lot of people find that they are much happier living in two inexpensive homes in two different areas (a winter home and a summer home). They say that it's more enjoyable than living in one more expensive home year round. We'll talk more about that lifestyle in a later chapter.

Searching Craigslist

I've set up a page on BestOf55Plus.com to show you the best results from craigslist so you can get an idea of what is available and what the general prices are in the area you're interested in.

BestOf55Plus.com/craigslist

Find the area you're interested in, then scroll through the gallery and click on any home that looks interesting to you. Then you will see more information and more pictures. The next step is to actually physically go look at the homes.

Even if you are not ready to make a decision yet and just want some general information, searching Craigslist will quickly give you an idea of what is available in your price range. I think you will be pleasantly surprised at how much house you can get for your money.

Searching eBay

BestOf55Plus.com also has a section to search eBay at: *BestOf55Plus.com/ebay*

One other thing you can do with an eBay search is to choose "Completed Listings." This will tell you what homes actually sold for instead of what owners are asking for the homes.

By doing a little research you will be better informed to recognize a good deal when you start physically looking at homes.

Price Isn't Everything

Of course, be sure to check on the HOA fees and
the rules before you get too serious about any home.
When you do get serious about a home, be sure to
check out all of the items listed next in the Buyer
Checklist.

Chapter 7

Buyer Checklist

Below is my list of the things you need to be sure to check off before you buy a home in a 55+ park.

Note that not everything has to pass, but, if it doesn't, and you buy the home, you want it to be because you considered a fault or problem and decided that you could fix it or that it wasn't important to you.

What you don't want to happen is to find out after you buy the home that there was something that you forgot to check.

After you have checked everything on the list and made a note of anything on the list that is a problem, then you can look at the items on the list that are problems and decide whether to try to get the owner to fix the problem or perhaps you will decide that it's not a big deal. And, of course, you can use the problem items in your negotiating to get the price down.

One final thought. There are some things on the list that you may consider deal killers. If you find any of these, you can stop your checking at that point and go on to look at the next home. I have put the deal killers at the top of the list so you don't waste a lot of time checking other things and then find that there is a deal killer for you near the bottom of the list.

Here's my Buyer Checklist

I will start with the six things that I consider to be deal killers for me. You might be a little more tolerant on a few of the items than I would but, personally, I don't want to deal with these problems right off the bat when I buy a home.

If some of these problems show up after I have moved into the house, I will deal with them then, but for me there are too many good homes on the market that don't have any of these problems.

Deal-Killing Items to Check

Mildew

This is especially important to look for when buying a home in Florida. It may not be much of a problem in Arizona, but in Florida it can be. Mildew can be almost impossible to get rid of and it can be very bad for your health. You don't have to see it. If you can smell it when you first walk in, it's there. Walk away. Be sure to check when you first walk in. Your nose will adjust to it quickly and you won't know it's there after a minute or two, so be observant when you first walk in.

By the way, if you don't think your nose will block out smells quickly, try this. Blindfold someone and then hold half of an orange, lemon or onion under their nose and ask them to identify the smell. They can almost always do this easily. Hold it there and ask them to tell you when you take it away. In less than a minute, they will usually say that it's gone. That's how fast your nose disregards strong smells. I guess it's nature's way of saying that if there is a strong smell and you can't do anything about it, you might as well ignore it.

If you can smell it when you first walk in, it's there. Walk away. Mildew is very bad for your health and is hard to get rid of. This would be a deal killer for me.

Has the home been smoked in?

For some people this is not a big deal, but for me it's a major concern and a deal killer. Be sure to consider this when you first walk in. As with mildew, you won't be able to detect it after your nose has adjusted to it.

Water damage

This can be expensive to repair and there may be a lot more damage than is first visible. Look for discoloration or stains on the ceiling. Look for stains around the windows.

Soft or spongy places in the floor could also be a sign of water damage. Be sure to check around the toilet and washing machine.

Mice

Look for signs of mice around the water heater and anywhere the water pipe comes into the home. Also, look around where the gas line comes in. Mice can do a lot of damage and getting rid of them can be hard and you can end up with a bad smell for a long time when you use poison to kill mice. Just walk away.

Title trouble

Make sure the seller has a clear title. A manufactured home, mobile home, or whatever you call it is considered more like a vehicle than a home. It has a VIN (Vehicle Identification Number) and a title. You have to pay the annual personal property tax and put a new sticker on it every year—at least, that's the law in most states.

If there is a small lien on a higher priced home, I might consider it, but for lower priced homes, it's not worth the hassle.

On a side note, if you are in financial trouble and are considering bankruptcy, Florida law says that your house cannot be taken in bankruptcy or to satisfy a judgment. But keep in mind that a manufactured home or mobile home is not considered to be a home. It is personal property and is not protected from seizure. (This is not legal advice—just my understanding of the law.)

Lies

Be wary if you catch the owner (or agent) not being truthful. If he will lie about one thing, he will lie about more things. Ask a few questions that you already know the answer to in order to see if he is truthful.

For example, when I was looking to buy the motorhome I live in now (I'll talk more about that later), I was looking at a motorhome that had nearly new tires on it. I asked the salesman how much a new set of six tires would cost and he said $4,000 to $5,000 or more. Motorhome tires are expensive, but not that expensive. $2,000 to $2,500 will buy a good set of tires. I didn't buy that motorhome because I no longer believed anything the salesman told me.

Finally, go with your gut. If a deal seems too good to be true, the deal just doesn't feel right, or you don't have a good feeling about the owner or sales agent, walk away.

There are a lot of great homes in 55+ parks on the market right now and in this market as a buyer with cash (or the ability to get financing), you are in the driver's seat.

Other Issues

These aren't necessarily deal-killers, but questions that should be on your Buyer Checklist

Who owns the land under the home?
In some parks, the association owns the land under the members' homes and in others the developer or an investor owns the land. Sometimes there is an agreement for the HOA to buy the land over a certain number of years.

I know of one small park where an older guy owned the park. He was a delightful gentleman in his 90s. It was his park and he ran it like a dictator. If you didn't like his rules, you could leave. Surprisingly, it was a smooth running park.

Later he sold it to the residents under an arrangement whereby the association would pay him a certain amount each month as long as he or his wife lived and then the association would own the land free and clear.

It was an interesting park. The owner lived on the property and in the house where he was born. His orange groves surrounded the park and residents were allowed pick all of the oranges they wanted for their own use.

After the association took over, it didn't run as smoothly. With 50 people all putting their two cents worth in, there never did seem to be as much harmony as there was when the old gentleman owned it. I hate to say it, but maybe in some cases a dictatorship is better than a democracy—at least for running a 55+ park.

Of course, most of the larger parks will have professional management and this won't be a problem.

Have there been any assessments or are any planned?

If so, when and how much? Some communities keep a reserve fund and some have the monthly fees set to just cover the basic month to month expenses and then they have an assessment every time there is a major expense—like the pool needs a new marcite coating or the clubhouse needs a new roof, etc.

Either way of managing the park is fine; you just need to know so you can compare the real expense of living in each park.

What percent of the residents are behind on their association dues?

With the recent downturn in the economy, some people have found themselves financially strapped. Maybe their house back home didn't sell as fast as they expected or maybe they have used some of their money to help out their children who have lost their jobs.

Whatever the reason, when some members get behind on their association dues, the association can find itself short on money. It may have to postpone some maintenance projects, cut back on services or even raise your dues to make up for the dues that are not being paid.

How old is the park?

One reason you might want to know the age of the park is that a rough, general rule is the older the park, the older the residents tend to be. For example, a park that is three years old will tend to have more residents in their late 50s and one that's 20 years old will tend to have more residents who are in their 70s and 80s. Of course, this is not always the case, but something to keep in mind.

The reason it might matter is that younger residents tend to me more active than older residents. If you're looking for a lot of activity and neighbors who like to get out and do things, you would want to be around the younger crowd. On the other hand, if you want to spend your time relaxing and being more laid back, you would be happier in a less active community.

Your personal checklist

There may be other things that you want to add to your personal Buyer Checklist—in other words, things that are important to you when selecting a house. Here are some more things that might be on your personal Buyer Checklist:

- The size of the yard.

- How close is it to the street (and noise)?

- How new are the appliances?

- Will the carpet need to be replaced soon?

- What is the view from your screened-in porch? Will you be looking into a wooded area or at your neighbor's trash can?

I'm sure you will decide to add more items to your checklist, but this is a start. Make pictures and keep good notes as you do your searching. After you look at a few homes, the details will all start running together. Don't depend on your memory unless you are only looking at a very few homes.

Armed with this checklist, you are ready to start your search. Enjoy the adventure.

Chapter 8

Homeowner Associations

The homeowner's association (HOA) is like the government of your 55+ park. Like a town, your HOA provides services, collects taxes in the form of fees, and has its own set of laws, the park rules. You'll want to know all you can about the way the HOA works on paper and how that translates into the real world.

How much is the HOA (Homeowner Association) fee and what does it cover?

A low HOA fee is not always a good thing. Just like you'd think twice before moving to a city with low property taxes but no money in the budget for the police department or trash collection, you need to check and see what you get for what you pay.

Also keep in mind that HOA fees are almost sure to go up; I don't know of a case where they ever went down. If you are on a fixed income and they go up substantially, that could be a problem. In some cases HOA fees can go up by only a defined amount in a year. This is spelled out on the HOA bylaws.

Most of the time they go up only to cover inflation, but members could vote to raise the fees to cover more services or better liability insurance, etc. And, of course, if there are more hurricanes, tornadoes or floods in the area, the insurance will likely go up.

If the value of the property goes up, the insurance for the clubhouse, etc. will go up. Taxes could go up, too.

Here's another example of why HOA fees could go up. If the majority of the members decided that they wanted to change the park to a gated community, putting 24-hour guards at the gate could get expensive. Even buying the equipment required to have an automated gate would be somewhat costly.

Here's another example. The board may decide that the reserve fund is not large enough to cover the new clubhouse roof that's going to be needed in the next few years. HOA fees will need to be raised to keep from having an assessment.

Any of the things discussed above will likely result in HOA fees going up.

One of the things you should check out is how much is in the reserve fund now and whether it is enough to cover any anticipated upcoming expenses.

If you're on a tight budget, the increase in HOA fees required to cover these expenses could be a big strain on your budget. And, of course, an assessment could really be a jolt to your budget.

Bottom line, keep in mind that HOA fees can – and probably will – go up over time. Budget for this.

Here is a list of items that are sometimes included and sometimes not.

- **Basic maintenance of the common areas** is almost always included. Water, sewerage and garbage pickup are usually included. Also, use of the pool is usually included, but not the golf course—if there is one on the property. The rest of the things on this list are sometimes included and sometimes not. Be sure to find out.

- **Yard mowing**. Of course, the common area mowing will be included but, in some cases, the HOA fee will include mowing individual yards. Even if the mowing of your private yard is not included, there is usually no shortage of individuals and companies who will mow your small yard for a very reasonable charge.

- **Cable TV**. Sometimes it's just very basic service and sometimes it covers a much better package.

If your HOA fee covers cable TV, be sure to check and see what the package consists of.

- **Free Wi-Fi**. A lot of parks are now starting to include free Wi-Fi. It may not be as fast as you want, but if you're just checking email and doing a little surfing, it may be all you need. Be sure to check the signal strength at the home you are thinking about buying. Sometimes there is not a strong signal in all parts of the park.

- **A monthly catered get-together** paid for by the association is sometimes included. Practically all parks have a monthly or quarterly pot-luck dinner for the people who want to participate.

- **Pest Control**. Most HOAs cover monthly inspections and pest control.

- **Snow removal**. Yes, some people want to retire to places where there can be snow—not me.

- **An outside post light** (like a little street light) for each home is sometimes included. Sometimes these are connected to the residence's electricity and sometimes they are all wired to the same electricity as the clubhouse, meaning the association pays that bill.

Usually it's the homeowner's obligation to do minor maintenance—keep the pole painted black and replace the light bulb when it burns out. Of course, sometimes the association takes care of this. It depends on what the rules stipulate. Either way, it's no big deal, but you would like to know so that six months after you move in you don't get a letter from the association telling you that your light pole needs painting.

The Rules

Ask for an up-to-date copy of the rules and regulations.

It's very important that you have this before you make a decision on any park or home. The rules may be too strict for you or they may not be strict enough. And there may be one or more of the rules that are deal killers for you.

What do the rules say about pets? There may be rules that say things like only two pets are allowed or no dogs over 50 pounds, etc. If you have a 55 pound dog or have three cats, this rule would be a deal killer for you. You don't want to find this out after you have bought the home. Of course, if you don't have pets or don't like pets, you might love this rule.

How strictly are the rules enforced?
You will have to ask around to find out about this. How strictly do you want them to be enforced? Do you want common sense to play a part in the enforcement?

For example, my parents lived in a place where the rules said that only two guests could be at the pool at any one time. They never used the pool themselves, but once every year or so, their three great-grandkids would come to visit.

Mother would take all three of the kids to the pool. That was against the letter of the law, but no one ever said anything about it. My mother was adamant. She said, "I use the pool one hour every two years and I'm not going to tell my grandkids that only two of them can go to the pool at a time."

I think this is an example of where common sense rather than strict enforcement of the rules made sense.

In another case I know of, there was a situation in a small park that created a lot of ill-will. Most of the residents were there during only the winter months, but some stayed there year-round. The park wasn't on city sewer. There was one big septic system for the whole park. It worked fine and there was never a problem, but for years the association had enforced the rule that there could be no washing machines in the homes because they didn't think the sewer system would handle all of the extra water.

There were washers and dryers in a central location and they were connected to a separate new sewer system.

The members constantly voted not to spend the money it would take to put in a new sewer system— which would necessitate a substantial increase in the HOA fees or an assessment. They were happy with things the way they were.

One summer, while many residents were gone, one lady had a washer and dryer installed in her home. When everyone got back, someone found out about it and it came up at a board meeting. The lady said she had trouble walking (which she did) and she said she wasn't able to walk to the laundromat.

It caused some heated discussions in the member meetings. Several people were saying that they had trouble walking too. The end result was that she had to take her washer out. Some decisions are not easy. One washer wouldn't have caused any trouble with the septic system, but 50 would have.

Professional management

Having to make decisions like this is one reason that sometimes it's better to have a professional manager instead of having the members handle the day to day decisions.

A professional manager would have been better in the above situation involving the washing machine. A professional manager could have handled the situation instead of the lady's friends voting to tell her that she had to remove her washing machine.

Get the inside story

Ask people in the park what they like and dislike about the park. Sometimes you can get some really helpful information and get a good or bad feeling about the park.

Of course, if you have a particular home you're considering, it's always good to meet some of the neighbors. You can ask them what they like and dislike about the park and ask them if they know anything about the home. Did the previous owners take good care of it? Has there been any water damage, etc.?

Value for your money

Keep in mind that having a lot of services included in the HOA fee can be a good deal. Usually it would be a lot cheaper for the association to negotiate a rate to cover the whole park for services such as cable TV, Wi-Fi, yard mowing, pest control, etc. than it would be for everyone to contract individually for all of these services.

Sometimes an increase in the HOA fee can be a good thing if you get something worthwhile in return. For example, if the HOA fee goes up $40 a month to cover free cable TV and you get to stop paying the cable company $90 a month then this will actually save you money and help your monthly budget.

Chapter 9

Ways to Earn Money without a Computer

If you had an extra million dollars, would that make your retirement a lot more enjoyable and less stressful?

If you had a million dollars in the bank, you would be hard-pressed to draw $30,000 a year or $2,500 a month interest payments from your million in the bank. In this chapter and the next one, I'm going to show you several ways you could make $2,500 a month after you retire with little or no up-front investment.

I'm not going to try to cover all of the ways you could make extra money; I'm only going to try to cover some ways to make money that you may not have thought about. Many of the ideas I will present will be considered outside-the-box or non-conventional.

When you're thinking about living in a 55+ park, having just a little bit of extra money can make life a lot more enjoyable. That's true regardless of your budget.

Even $500 extra spendable income a month would allow you to live in a much nicer home. It would allow you to own or lease a nice car. It would allow you to go on a cruise every few months, and the list goes on and on. And of course, it would allow a couple to eat out several times a week.

After thinking about all of the things $500 extra a month would allow you to do, you might decide that you want to make $1,000 a month. I think you will see that the $2,500 a month number we just talked about is easily within your reach.

One thing to keep in mind is that, after you find a fun way to make extra money, in most cases, you can work more or less and make more or less. You are in control.

I won't be going into a lot of detail on each technique. In most cases, a book could be written on each technique and, in most cases, it has. In fact, I will point you toward some of these books, videos and websites.

As an added bonus, most of the money-making techniques I describe here will get you out of the house and have you out meeting people. Some of them may even allow you to get some useful exercise. At the very least, they will help keep you active.

The following information is mainly a list with a brief description of the pros and cons of the technique. Let's start with ways to make money without a computer or the Internet.

First of all, make sure to check the rules and bylaws of your park and make sure that what you plan to do doesn't violate the rules.

I'm sure there are several ways to make money that you have thought about, such as getting a part-time job, etc. In the following list, I'm going to give you some ideas that you probably haven't thought of. Be open minded. Don't automatically dismiss the ideas and say, "Oh, that wouldn't work for me."

Here's the list of ways to make money that you probably haven't thought of yet:

Be a Visiting Angel™

Visiting Angel™ is a national company (and, from what I've heard, they provide a great service). In any 55+ park, I'm sure you can find several people who need a little help.

You could go in for an hour or so a day, make sure they have taken their medication, maybe fix a meal, do laundry, wash dishes, help them pay bills, drive them to the store or do some grocery shopping for them, make doctor appointments, etc.

And, of course, one of the most important things you could do would be to just visit, talk to the person, and listen. Give them someone to talk to on a daily basis.

A lot of people could get by a lot longer without having to go into a nursing home if they had just a little help. It's expensive to hire this kind of help but, in your case, you could do the work for a lot less than a professional service because you would just be walking around the corner.

Of course, you could perform the service in nearby 55+ parks also.

I have a friend who has done this for years. She says it's enjoyable work and she feels very much appreciated.

Her clients are wealthy and live in large homes that they don't want to leave. With her help, they can stay in their homes. So you might also look for clients in nearby areas other than in the 55+ park where you live.

Give music lessons

You don't have to be an expert musician to be a good teacher. In fact, most experts are not good teachers. Do you think Elton John would be the best piano teacher? Whether it's keyboard, guitar, banjo, fiddle, dulcimer, the list goes on and on. If you teach beginners, you have to know only a little more than your students to be a good teacher.

To be a good music teacher, you have to know the song you're teaching in your conscious mind and in your sub-conscious mind. Most musicians only know songs in their sub-conscious mind.

For example, even if you're not into bluegrass music, you have probably heard of Dr. Ralph Stanley who played and sang several of the songs in the movie, *O Brother, Where Art Thou?* By the way, Ralph is 87 and still going strong. He is touring and performing almost every week.

Ralph is a great banjo player. When you're playing the banjo, there are times where you do what is called a "pull-off," where a finger on your left hand pulls off of a string after you have picked the string with a finger on your right hand.

You can do this by either pulling a finger down or flicking it up. Either way gives you the same sound and some players do it one way and some do it the other way.

I was talking to Ralph one day at a bluegrass festival. By the way, he's very willing to talk to fans and beginning musicians. I asked him whether he did a pull-down or a flip up on a song that I'm sure he has played thousands of times. He said, "I don't know. Let me get my banjo out and I will see."

Even though he had played the song thousands of times, his conscious mind didn't know what his hands were doing. His sub-conscious mind did. Some people call this "muscle memory." Anyway, I think you get the point. Being a beginner could actually be a benefit when teaching other beginners.

Don't automatically dismiss this idea if you like to play an instrument.

Teach almost anything you enjoy

You can make money teaching sewing, jewelry making, painting, photography, video, yoga, as a workout instructor, or teaching an exercise, swimming, canning, or cooking class.

In each of these areas, you can specialize. You could teach Cajun cooking, old time cooking, French cooking, etc.

I have a friend who teaches music (string instruments) and his wife teaches old time cooking— canning (green beans, tomatoes, etc.), making jams and preserves, making pickles, etc. They both have waiting lists for their classes.

Make jewelry and sell it

There are books, YouTube videos and workshops that will teach you how to do it. You won't get rich, but we're not talking about getting rich—we're talking about making $500 to $2,500 or so a month.

Babysit or pet sit

Be sure to check the rules and regulations regarding this. Even if there are rules against you doing pet sitting in your own home, a lot of people want their dogs to stay home and have someone come by a couple of times a day to feed them and take them for a walk. This would get you out of the house, allow you to get some exercise, and it wouldn't violate any rules.

Sell products at a trade show

I know people who have made $5,000 in three days at a trade show selling plans on how to build something. I have spent many weekends selling items at trade shows and you would be surprised at what you can sell at trade shows. I know a couple who go to at least one trade show a month. He sells cowboy hats and she sells gold and silver chains by the inch.

I have never sold a refrigerator to an Eskimo at a trade show, but I have sold sand to someone from Saudi Arabia. (It was a special kind of sand for swimming pool filters.)

Having a booth and selling at trade shows is profitable and, best of all, it's a lot of fun. I've done it off and on for years.

I know one lady who weaves baskets. It takes her about a day to make a big basket that she sells for $150. She told me that she goes to four craft fairs a year and she is able to sell all of the baskets she makes by going to those four shows. The best part is that she is making money doing something she loves to do.

Of course, what sells best depends on what kind of trade show it is. DVDs, CDs, LEDs, jewelry, paintings, soap, and all kinds of crafts are just some examples of things that sell well.

Ideally, you would like to have something that people can't find at Walmart or anywhere else when they get home. They have to buy it now or forever do without it.

You want something that's small and easy to take to the show. People want to pay for it and put it in their bag and leave with it.

Substitute teach

This is a great way to make $80 or so a day and you can choose when and how many days you want to work. In some states you are not even required to have a college degree or teaching experience to do substitute teaching.

Teach at a community college

If you have a college degree, you could teach one or two courses a semester at a local community college. The classes are usually at night, but not always. It's interesting work and a lot of people enjoy it. My brother and his wife did it for years after they retired.

I have a friend who is 76. He teaches one course each semester at a major university. The subject he teaches is entrepreneurship. He put his own course together and there is always a waiting list to get into his classes.

Universities are now offering degrees and training in non-conventional areas. A friend of mine recently received her master's degree and her major was crisis management.

I have a cousin who is working on her master's degree in education technology. I can see a need for this type of information being taught, but I never thought about someone being able to get a master's degree in that field.

The University of Memphis offers a degree in sales. Most business schools have marketing classes, but Memphis is the only college I know of that offers a degree in sales.

Bottom line: If you have a unique talent or interest, you might be surprised at how open a university would be to putting a non-traditional course in their curriculum and letting you teach it.

There are a lot more unusual or non-traditional courses being taught at community colleges or technical colleges than at major universities, so I would suggest that you look into these first. Start by picking up one of their course catalogs and see what is being offered now and see if there are any of those courses that you would like to teach.

Offer an off-season home-watch service for snowbirds

By a "home-watch service," I don't mean that you would offer to go by people's homes and fix their watches. I'm talking about watching homes for people while they're away.

People who live in a 55+ community live only part of the year are referred to as snowbirds. You could offer a service to check on their homes every month or every week. You could check for storm damage, water leaks, run the AC (it's not good for air conditioners to sit idle for months at a time—the seals dry out). And, of course, you would check for signs of break-ins or if anything seem to be missing or disturbed.

You could offer inside and outside inspection services or outside only. You could offer this service on a weekly, by-weekly or monthly basis.

In the next chapter I will talk about how to make extra money with your computer and the Internet.

Keep in mind that you don't have to choose just one money-making endeavor. You can make money with your computer and without. I do both.

Chapter 10

How to Make Money with Your Computer

Craigslist

One thing that a lot of people do to make money is to buy and sell items on Craigslist. Stick to items you know something about and are interested in.

Some of the things people are buying and selling are musical instruments, tractors, appliances, bicycles, cars, trucks, motorhomes, antiques, and the list goes on and on.

My mother bought a vase for 50 cents at a garage sale and sold it on eBay for $75. She bought a hand-painted plate for a dime and sold it for $114.50. Of course, she knew the value of antiques and recognized a bargain when she saw it.

My father's rule (that I go by all the time) is that, "You make your money when you buy it—not when you sell it." He said that you can sometimes sell something for more than it's worth, but don't bet your business on being able to do that.

Amazon

One of the money-making techniques I use is selling items on Amazon. I do this in two ways.

The first way is that I go to Walmart, ToysRUs, Bed Bath and Beyond, and other retail stores and find closeout items or other deeply discounted items that I can sell on Amazon.

I use an app on my cell phone to read the bar code and then I can immediately see what the item is selling for on Amazon.

I usually try to find items that I can get a 3 to 1 markup on. For example, if I see that an item is selling on Amazon for $60, I don't buy it unless I can buy it for about $20 or less. You need this markup to make money. You will have to pay Amazon a 15% fee and you will have to pay shipping to the customer.

You really can find items with this kind of markup and you can do it every day. I recently bought 50 toys for $29.95 each and sold them for $159 to $169 each. You don't find these kinds of deals every day, but they're out there. Usually, I can only get two or three items when I find them on clearance.

When I work hard at it, I can usually sell $1,000+ a day and clear about a third of that.

The China connection

The other way I make money with Amazon is that I buy items from China (usually 100 to 1,000 at a time). I buy through Alibaba Express or Alibaba, which is a Chinese company that is planning on doing an IPO and appearing on one of the US stock exchanges soon.

I place my order directly with one of the thousands of companies that they represent. Then I give them my credit card number and they charge my account and hold the money in escrow until I receive the items that I ordered and tell them that I'm satisfied with the delivery. Then they release the money to the supplier.

I have been doing this for about a year now and have never had a problem.

Your money is tied up longer this way, but you can usually double your money in about 90 days. Of course, sometimes you make a mistake and buy an item that doesn't sell as well as you thought it would.

I bought some spatulas that I had to sell at just over my cost to get rid of them. I didn't lose any money, but I didn't make anything much on that order.

I also bought 100 aprons that are not selling well. So you win some and you lose some. I try to buy items from China at a price where I can at least double my money and usually triple my money, after Amazon fees.

I have ordered items from China on Monday and received them on Wednesday (I guess an airplane can only fly so fast), but it usually takes about a week to get my order.

I always buy items with the shipping included in the price.

When I have 100 or 1,000 units of an item, I ship them to Amazon and use their FBA (Fulfill by Amazon) service. Amazon takes the orders, ships the merchandise and handles all of the customer service. Then they deposit money into my bank every two weeks.

They charge more for this service. They charge about 35% instead of the 15% they charge when I do the shipping.

By the way, I recommend that you only buy about 100 of an item until you test it and find out that it sells well.

Be sure to negotiate when you are dealing with Chinese companies. Actually, negotiate when you are dealing with any supplier.

I have found that the Chinese suppliers will usually come down about 30% to 35%. All negotiating is done by email and they are 12 hours ahead of Eastern Time, so 9:00 pm to 10:00 pm Eastern Time is 9:00 am to 10:00 am their time. You will usually get a quick response if you send email messages at this time.

There are a lot of books on Amazon that go into details about how do both the Walmart and the China technique.

If you think you would enjoy making money this way, be sure to start small and learn what you're doing before you invest a lot of money.

By the way, for Chinese items, I like to find items that will sell between $10 and $50. For Walmart items, I like to find items that sell in the $30 to $300 range.

With the Walmart items, you usually have 90 days to take something back if it doesn't sell, but that's not the case with the Chinese items.

I don't buy anything from China that you plug into the wall or put in your mouth.

Of course, read Amazon's rules and make sure you follow them exactly or you could have your account closed and you can't just go set up another account.

For example, if a customer asks a question, you have to respond within 24 hours. And when you answer the question and the customer replies with a "Thank you," you have to answer that too. You can click a box that says, "No response required," but you can't just ignore the customer's comment. This is just one example of the many Amazon rules you have to strictly follow.

After all, Amazon has plenty of sellers. They want more buyers and they sure don't want to make a customer mad. If a customer wants to return an item and gives as his reason, "I changed my mind" or "I found it cheaper," you have to take it back. It's just part of the cost of doing business. Accept it and go on.

Some people laugh at the things I sell on Amazon. I have sold toilet seats, sewing machines, gloves, tents, toys, and the list goes on and on.

Subscription websites

Another way I make money with my computer and the Internet is with subscription websites. Subscription websites are kind of like magazine subscriptions. People pay a monthly fee to be a member of the site and I write new articles each week.

To be successful with a subscription website, you would need to select a topic that you know a lot about—and, of course, a topic that people are willing to pay a monthly fee for to get the information.

Here are two of my subscription websites:

MarketingYourRestaurant.com

SearchEngineU.com

The software I use to run these sites is MemberGate. You can find it at *MemberGate.com.*

Ad-supported websites

One more way I make money by using my computer is that I have ad-supported websites. I have about 25 now. I used to have 250. I put these sites up and then I don't have to do anything with them. They just bring in cash year after year—not much, of course, but by having several of them the income adds up.

Some people place Amazon ads on their sites and Amazon pays them when someone clicks on the ads. I just put eBay ads on my sites and eBay changes the list of auctions all the time to keep the site up to date. I don't do anything.

I received a check from eBay for $1,700 one month, but that was back before they changed their rules. They don't pay as much now. The good part is that I put these sites up several years ago and I haven't touched them since and they are still bringing in a small check every month. The key is to have websites with information that people are interested in. Below is one of my eBay ad supported websites.

UsedTractorReviews.com

Books and videos

Writing books and producing DVDs is another way to make money with your computer. Novels outsell 'How To' books by about 100 to 1, but writing novels is not my expertise. I have eight books that are being sold on Amazon. None of them are novels. If they were, I would be making a lot more money.

Yet another way to make money with your computer is to have websites where you sell physical products. Below is a link to a website where I have been selling novelty million dollar bills for over 10 years.

zMillionDollar.com

My approach is to have several streams of income. I don't depend on just one way of making money on the Internet.

One website I highly recommend you check out to learn about product development is Bill Myers' site at www.Bmyers.com. It's a subscription website. It costs $9.95 a month and you can cancel at any time. I have been a member for more than 10 years and have learned a lot from Bill.

There's a wealth of project, product and money making ideas on the site and new information is added several times a week. There is also a lively discussion forum on the site.

Fiverr.com

One final way to make money using your computer and the Internet is to do work on *Fiverr.com.*

This is a website (as the name implies) where you charge $5 to perform a service. They call $5 worth of service a "gig." You might think that you can't make money doing tasks for $5 each, but the key is that you offer (and usually get) extras added to your gigs.

You can offer to finish the work in one day instead of three for $5 or $10 extra. You can offer to include a different view if you're doing graphic design work and you can even list an extra saying that you accept tips.

What kind of work do people do on Fiverr? One example is the cover of this book. I paid someone $5 to design the front cover. I paid $5 extra to have the designer send me a 3D image (which took the designer almost no time at all).

I have written eight books and I have used Fiverr to have all of my book covers designed.

Here are some other services you can offer on Fiverr:

- Proofreading – I have used this service. You offer to proofread one chapter or a certain number of words for the basic $5 fee

- Voice overs

- Use PhotoShop to touch up a photo

- Design a logo

- Write a testimonial

- Make a video testimonial

There are literally hundreds of categories of services you can provide. Go to www.Fiverr.com and check them out. I bet you will find several services you can offer.

While you're on the site, go through the steps and become a gig provider in one or more categories and give it a try.

I won't try to cover all of the details about how to make money using Fiverr in this book. A whole book could be written about the topic. In fact, I just did a search on Amazon and found that 261 books have been written about how to make money using Fiverr. Of course, you can learn a lot by just visiting their website at www.Fiverr.com.

One of the newest books on the topic and one of the highest rated ones is, *The Fiverr Masters Class*. You'll find links to it and other Fiverr resources at:

BestOf55Plus.com/fiverr

Chapter 11

Alternative I – Living full-time in a motorhome

I have experienced living in 55+ retirement parks. I also lived in Costa Rica for six months. I now live full-time in a 34-foot motorhome. This picture of my present home was taken when I pulled into a Cracker Barrel restaurant for lunch recently.

I enjoyed all three options. They each have their advantages and disadvantages. In this chapter I'm going to discuss motorhome living. In the following chapter I will discuss living in Costa Rica.

First of all, if you are even remotely thinking about living full-time (or even part-time) in a motorhome, by all means read *Buying a Used Motorhome: how to get the most for your money and not get burned* by Bill Myers.

You can get the Kindle version for $2.99 or the paperback version for $13.46. Find the books and other resources at the link below:

BestOf55Plus.com/rv

There are between 250,000 and 7 million people living full-time in motorhomes (depending on how you define full-time and which experts you listen to).

For example, there are a lot of people who live in a motorhome full-time—part of the time. They live in their motorhome during the winter or during the summer. Are these people full-timers? It depends on your definition of the term 'full-time'.

Anyway, let's just say that there are a lot of people who live the RV lifestyle. By the way, in this chapter I am going to use the terms "RV" and "Motorhome" interchangeably because they are used this way by most people.

Technically, a motorhome is a type of RV. A boat and an off-road vehicle are RVs also.

A lot of people think of living in a motorhome as being on the road all the time. Some people do that, but most people stay at one campground for few days or even a few weeks—sometimes for months.

The average motorhome is driven 3,500 miles a year. That's about 300 miles a month, which is why, if you look at a 10 year-old motorhome, it will likely have about 35,000 miles on it.

Here are the pros, cons, and things to consider:

The Pros:

- Freedom. You can live where you want to and move with the seasons. You are not tied down. You can change your mind tonight and live somewhere else tomorrow night. And you can change your mind and sell your RV and live a different lifestyle in a heartbeat.

- If you change your mind, you can sell a motorhome in a matter of weeks instead of the months or years it can take to sell a house.

- If you don't like your neighbors, you can move in a matter of minutes.

- You can enjoy international travel and not have to still be paying living expenses back home while you're gone. Just put your RV in storage at $50 a month.

- When I was between houses, condos, and RVs, I spent six months in Costa Rica. It was a fun and interesting experience (which I will talk about in the next chapter). It was inexpensive, but it wouldn't have been so inexpensive if I were paying for rent (or a mortgage payment), electricity, cable TV, Internet, taxes, etc. back home. When you're living in a motorhome, you have the freedom to almost totally eliminate expenses back home while you travel abroad. Whether you ever want to do it or not doesn't matter. Just having the freedom to do it is a good feeling.

- Having everything you need handy is one thing I really like. When I first started living full-time in a motorhome I found it funny that, a time or two, when I was getting ready to take a trip, I would catch myself thinking about what I needed to pack. Then I would realize that I didn't have to pack. Everything I own was going with me.

The Cons:

I had a hard time finding things to list in this section because I like almost everything about motorhome living—but that's just me. Here are some things that may be considered cons for some people:

- You don't have as much privacy in campgrounds.

- Sometimes there are noises such as barking dogs, motorhomes pulling in and out, etc.

- You won't have your friends nearby to enjoy and spend time with. It's easy to make new friends in campgrounds, but many of them are gone within a week or two.

- Your grandkids may not be close by and, if they come to visit you in the summer, it can get crowded after a short while. Of course, they would probably enjoy it—at least for a while. It would be an adventure for them, and where you are this summer may be different from where you were last summer.

- Your regular doctors may not be close by.

Other Things to Consider:

- If you have a partner, do you both really want this lifestyle?

- Do you get along well enough with each other to spend a lot of time in close quarters?

- Do you both have hobbies, interests or things you really like to do that don't involve the other person—reading, writing, knitting, crafts, computers, etc.?

- Do you have things or people back 'home' that you need to look after or take care of—rental property, aging parents, etc.?

Resources

If you want to work and be a full-time RVer, check out the website below:

WorKamper.com

One couple told me that they select work they want to do using the Workamper™ website. They get free camping and they get paid. Here are some of the jobs they have had in the last year or so:

Tram driver, interpreter, campground host, pointing out eagles and other wildlife at a national park, guest services and maintenance at a resort ranch

You would be surprised at all of the work options you can find at the *WorKamper.com* website.

To get a feel of what it's like to live full-time in a motorhome (or RV as they are also called), visit the website *RVnet.com* and check out their discussion forum.

You can also check out *RV-Dreams.com*

I keep an updated list of the best resources for RV living at *BestOf55Plus.com/rv*

Cost

The cost of living full-time in a motorhome can be about the same or maybe even less than living in a 55+ park.

Typical manufactured homes in a 55+ park will run between $10,000 and $50,000. Of course, you can go much higher than this.

Likewise, the typical cost of a used motorhome will run between $10,000 and $50,000. Again, you can spend a lot more than $50,000 on a used motorhome. Many of the later model, fancy motorhomes can easily run upwards of $100,000, particularly the diesel rigs.

These are usually referred to as diesel pushers or DP because the engine is in the back. In that sense, I guess it is pushing the motorhome instead of pulling it if the engine is in the front like the typical gasoline engines are.

The diesel engines will run well over half a million to a million miles and the Ford V-10 gasoline engine (which is now used in all gasoline RVs) will easily go 200,000 to 300,000 miles with no problem.

You will wear out everything in the RV way before you'll have any trouble with either engine. In fact, be leery of a used motorhome with very low mileage. Setting up and not being driven for months at a time can cause a lot of maintenance problems for a motorhome.

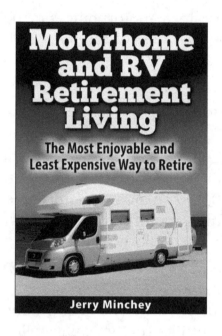

Find out more in Jerry's book about RV retirement

All of this and more is covered in Bill Myers' book discussed earlier in this chapter. As I said before, don't even think about buying a motorhome before you invest $2.99 for Bill's book.

Back to the cost of living full-time in a motorhome... The fee for campsites (like the HOA fees at 55+ parks) is a major expense and can be quite high or very reasonable.

For example, if you book a camping space for a month or more, you can stay in some very nice campgrounds for $350 to $450 a month. This includes electricity, Wi-Fi, water, sewerage, and sometimes cable TV is included.

In other words, you can spend $35,000 for a nice Class A motorhome with two slides (to give you plenty of room inside) and then $400 a month and is all you will have to spend, except for your food, medical expenses and insurance, which you will have to pay for wherever you live.

There will be some maintenance expenses and gas expenses if you do a lot of traveling.

Keep in mind that the $35,000 for a motorhome is just an example. Just as with homes in 55+ parks, you can find some nice motorhomes in the $15,000 to $25,000 range—it just takes a bit of searching.

Everyone thinks that the cost of gas is a major expense with a motorhome and it is if you travel almost every day or travel back and forth across the country, which some people do.

But if you stay in one campground for a month and then travel 300 miles to another one, this would add up to 3,600 miles a year. As we discussed earlier, this is about average for most people who are full-time RVers.

Let's do the math. Assume that you drive 3,600 miles a year and are getting nine miles per gallon. Some RVs get 8mpg and some get 10 mpg. How fast you drive will affect your mileage, but these numbers are in the ballpark.

That would mean that you would use 400 gallons of gas a year and, at $3.50 a gallon, that would be $1,400 a year for gas, or $117 a month. You're probably spending more than $117 a month on gas now in your present lifestyle.

As you can see in the above comparison of the numbers, living full-time in a motorhome and living in a 55+ park will cost you about the same. So cost is not really an issue. It comes down to which lifestyle you would enjoy the most.

Selling an RV or a home in a 55+ park can both be done fairly easily in a matter of a week or two, or a month or two at most, so with either lifestyle you choose, you are not locked in. You can change in a heartbeat and, if you do your homework and find a great deal (and do a good job of negotiating), you can likely sell your RV or 55+ home for more than you paid for it.

I have a friend who sells his RV and buys a different used one about twice a year. He looks for bargains and then lists his present RV on eBay and sells it in less than a week. He makes a profit almost every time. Sometimes he gets one of the largest Class A motorhomes and sometimes he goes with the little van-type Class B motorhomes. He says he enjoys the change and looking for bargains.

I like the idea of keeping the same RV. I do the same thing with cars. I usually keep a car for 10 years or more.

I'm not trying to talk you into living full-time in a motorhome. I'm just giving you the information so you can make an informed decision. Some people love the lifestyle but I also know some people who say that they could never be happy living like that.

If you can't decide whether you would like to live in a 55+ park or live full-time in a motorhome, you could do both. There are a lot (and I do mean a lot) of 55+ RV campgrounds.

Another option that we will talk about later is living in two different places. You could have a winter home and a summer home. You could go this route and one of your homes could be an RV. As explained in a later chapter about living in two places, it's not as expensive as you would think.

Want to know more?

If the idea of living full-time in a motorhome intrigues you in the least and you want to know more about it, take a look at my latest book that will be available through Amazon in both ebook and paperback in mid August, 2014. It's called:

Motorhome and RV Retirement Living: The Most Enjoyable and Least Expensive Way to Retire

This book goes into a lot more detail on the pros and cons of the motorhome and RV lifestyle than what I've included in this chapter.

The lifestyle is not right for everyone, but if you're even remotely considering it, you will find this book helpful and informative.

It will help you decide if motorhome living really is the lifestyle for you.

Chapter 12

Alternative II – Living in Costa Rica

A few years ago I lived in Costa Rica for six months. Actually, I stayed for three months and came home for Christmas to be with family and then went back for another three months. You can only stay in Costa Rica for three months at a time as a tourist.

If you decide to live there full-time, you can become a resident. That's not the same as being a citizen.

A lot of people become a 'permanent tourist.' They stay three months, catch a bus to Panama for three days (or fly back to the US) and then they are legal for another three months.

You don't have to speak Spanish to live there. I was hoping that I would improve my Spanish while I was there, but it's so easy to get by without Spanish that I didn't make much progress.

Living in Costa Rica is surprisingly inexpensive. The first time I was there I rented an almost new home for $900 a month and that included everything.

The house is owned by David and Marcia Murray. Dave has a small house that he built and lived in while he built his larger house next to it. Now he rents the small house out by the week or month.

You can learn more about renting Dave's house by visiting his website at *EnjoyCostaRica.co* and note that the suffix is "co" (for Costa Rica) and not "com." To contact him, click on the "contact" link on his website. At this writing, his rates are $275 for a week and $900 for a month and that includes everything.

On my second trip, I rented an apartment that was part of a new house. No one had ever lived there before. The price was $550 a month for the apartment and that included electricity, cable TV with US stations and a phone (with free calls to anywhere in Costa Rica).

Resources

You can learn more about the place I stayed by visiting their website at *Escape-in-Costa-Rica.com.*

To learn more about renting (or buying) other real estate in Costa Rica, I suggest you visit Scott Oliver's website, *WeLoveCostaRica.com.* It's a membership site and you have to sign up, but it's free.

When you get to his site, be sure to look in the left nav. panel and, under the Real Estate heading, click on the Rentals Long/Short Term link and you will find pictures and prices of several properties that are available for rent. I would highly recommend that you rent for a while before you consider moving there. There is a lot you need to know about the process of moving to and living in Costa Rica and, of course, you might not even like living there.

Also, be sure to check out the discussion forum on Scott's website. You can find a wealth of information there and you can ask any question you like. It's a great place to get your questions answered about visiting and living in Costa Rica. Just reading some of the previous questions and comments will provide you with a wealth of information.

I keep an updated list of websites and other Costa Rica information for you at:

BestOf55Plus.com/costa-rica

Life in Costa Rica

I didn't rent a car on either visit. Costa Rica has a network of new Mercedes buses and you can go any-where for about $1 an hour. A 20 minute ride into town was about 40 cents.

The local customs are different from the US in several interesting ways. For example, even though where I stayed (near the little town of Grecia) there was cof-fee growing as far as I could see in all directions, if I wanted a second cup of coffee at a restaurant I had to pay for a second cup. You don't get free coffee refills in Costa Rica like you do in the US.

Food was cheap. A big meal was $2 to $3 dollars and that included the tax and tip. In Costa Rica, all menu prices include the tax and tip.

You have a lot of options on where to live in Costa Rica. There is the Pacific on the west side and the Gulf of Mexico on the east site. In between the two coasts the mountains rise above 8,000 feet.

On the TV where people are always winning free trips to Costa Rica (Wheel of Fortune comes to mind), they are always showing the beautiful beaches but, to me, the beaches in Costa Rica are not as nice as Florida beaches.

I stayed near the little town of Gracia. It is known for being the cleanest town in Latin America. Actually, I was up the mountain a little from Gracia, I was at about 4,500 feet.

Overall, I found Costa Rica to be a wonderful place to live. The food is good (and very low cost). You can't beat the scenery, the mountains and waterfalls are spectacular.

The roads are paved, but rough as can be except the main roads. Except for petty theft in downtown San Jose, it is very safe.

People in Costa Rica are very friendly. I was walking around in the little town of Gracia looking for a business that had been recommended to me. And, by the way, most streets don't have names and there are no numbers on the buildings, so finding places can be hard sometimes.

Anyway, I saw a woman sitting on her front porch as I passed by, she spoke to me and then I asked her if she could tell me how to get to the business I was looking for. She called her teenage son out of the house to the front porch and she told him to get in her truck and take me to where I was going. He did and he was very nice.

I was getting my hair cut one morning and the lady's husband came in and the three of us were talking for a while. Then he invited me to come have Sunday lunch with him and his family. No barber in the US has ever invited me to come have Sunday lunch.

And, believe it or not, they have excellent low-cost healthcare with many US-trained doctors. Many people go there to get dental work done because of the quality of the work and the extremely low cost.

On my second trip, I ate something in the Ft. Lauderdale airport and got a severe case of food poisoning. I know I didn't get it in Costa Rica because I got sick before I had even taken a bite in Costa Rica.

Pharmacists can prescribe medicine in Costa Rica. About 9:00 o'clock at night I got so sick I had to have some relief. I went to the drug store (which was still open). The pharmacist took me back in his office, gave me a shot and prescribed some pills and gave them to me. I think my total bill was $9 and that was nine US dollars.

He also gave me his cell phone number and told me that he lived right behind the pharmacy and that, if I didn't get better an a few hours, to give him a call and he would meet me at the drug store.

I started getting better almost immediately and by the next morning I was weak, but had no more signs of food poisoning.

The reason I don't live in Costa Rica now is that I enjoy being around family too much to be so far away. Wherever you live, that's something for you to consider.

Regardless of where and how you decide to spend your retirement, you might want to at least consider a visit to Costa Rica. You will love it and, who knows, you might just decide to live there—at least for part of the year.

Chapter 13

Alternative III – Living in two different places

How about a winter home and a summer home?

A lot of people like the idea of having a winter home and a summer home. The concept is not just for the rich; there are several ways you can do this very inexpensively.

My parents did this for 15 years. They had a home in Tennessee and a home in Florida. When they traveled from one home to the other they didn't even take their toothbrushes. Both homes were fully furnished, including their clothes.

The 55+ parks can be as expensive or as inexpensive as you want. Think about it. Take your budget and consider what kind of home you could afford if you only had one home and then consider cutting that in half and think about what kind of homes you could have if you had two.

Also, consider the fact that, if you have two homes, they don't have to be equal in value. In fact, most people who have two homes don't have two homes of equal value.

Most people I know who have two homes seem to split it about 75% and 25%. For example, with a $40,000 budget, they might have a $30,000 home and a $10,000 home. I have even seen it split 90/10. With a $100,000 budget you could have a $90,000 home and a $10,000 home.

Whatever price range you are considering, think about knocking 10% to 20% off of that price and buying a second home. It's not the right choice for everyone, but a lot of people have found that they love the two home lifestyle.

If you think you couldn't be happy in a small, low-priced home, think about it as an adventure. If you've ever rented a mountain cabin or a beach house for a week, it probably wasn't as big as your regular home, but I bet you enjoyed it.

In your 'vacation' home (as some people like to call it) you don't need or want a lot of space. And as you saw in other chapters, you can get a lot of house for very little money in a 55+ park.

And of course, if you decide that you don't like the arrangement, it's easy to sell your second home and maybe even make a little money if you were diligent in searching and finding a great deal when you bought it—and great deals are out there.

Think about what is important to you. Think about the lifestyle of spending winters in a warm climate.

The price of your home doesn't determine the enjoyment in your life.

Normally, when you think of living in a lot lower price home, you might think that you would be living in a bad or less desirable neighborhood, maybe even a high-crime area.

That's not the case when you live in a 55+ community. Even though the homes are usually very inexpensive, you are not living in a bad neighborhood. You will find that most of the people there are doing just what you're doing. They no longer need a big house; they want quality of life.

One way to start the process is to keep your present home and get a winter home in a warm climate and see how you like it. Your new home doesn't have to be expensive.

When my parents were first thinking about living in a 55+ park, they bought a small, one bedroom home in a 55+ park. They paid $5,700 for it. That's right, $5,700 for a home.

They lived there for two winters, fixed it up and then sold it for a good profit and then bought a much nicer place in the same park. They found out that they loved the idea of living in two places.

For several years they kept their main home in Tennessee, but they soon realized that they looked forward to going to their small home in Florida a lot more than they looked forward to going back to Tennessee.

Selling a home in a 55+ park is easy.

Many people there have friends who are always asking them, "Do you know of any homes for sale in the park where you live?"

Ownership changes quite often. Every year there are people who, for various reasons, don't come back. Their home is for sale. In fact, many times people know before they leave in the spring that they won't be coming back and they want to sell their home.

By keeping your eyes open you can find some great deals and move up to a larger or nicer home and still stay in the same park. In the 55+ parks, everyone knows almost everyone there. They are very close knit communities.

You will find that people in the parks are a lot friendlier than people are in most neighborhoods. Do you know who lives three houses down the street from you? You would if you lived in a 55+ community.

Right now I live in different places with my motorhome. I have already booked all of Jan and Feb (and part of Dec and March) to be in state parks on the beaches in Florida. You have to book early to get ahead of the snowbirds (or, I should say, the *other* snowbirds).

I spend a lot of time in the North Carolina mountains and love it here, but I also enjoy the Florida beaches in the winter. I talked more about the option of living in a motorhome in a previous chapter.

When we were younger, having a bigger and bigger house and more and more stuff was what life was all about—at least, it seemed that way. That's what we wanted to do back then, but think about whether that is what you really want to do for the rest of your life.

I like to look at life as an adventure; some people don't want anything to change. They want everything to stay just like it has always been, they want to keep doing the same thing over and over. There's comfort in that, but that's not me.

Of course, some people want a different lifestyle, but they never get around to making it happen. I don't think that describes you. If it did, you wouldn't have purchased this book.

Doing something different or going off into the 'unknown' is always a little scary, but the good thing about moving into a 55+ community is that (as I've said before) it is so easy to sell your home and go back to your previous life—or sell it and go on to something else like living in Costa Rica, living in a motorhome (I talked about those options in earlier chapters) or living in a different 55+ park.

You don't always have to do what you've always done.

You may not know if you would like a different lifestyle until you try it. Some people find that they don't like the 55+ park lifestyle.

I had an employee once who didn't like change at all. It used to be a joke around the office that, if we ever decided to paint her office, we would have to paint one wall and wait a week and then paint another wall and continue that process until all four walls had been painted. She couldn't handle a change as big as painting all four walls in one day.

As I mentioned before, I spent six months living in Costa Rica. When I tell people about this, many of them say, "Oh, I would love to do that," but to this day not a one of them has even visited Costa Rica. Many people just never get around to taking action.

It's like the old joke, "If two birds were sitting on a fence and one decided to fly off, how many would be left?" More than likely, there would still be two (if birds are like people).

Just because a bird decided to fly off, doesn't mean that he actually did it. We all decide to do things and then never get around to doing them. And, of course, there are a lot of things that people (me too) just never get around to deciding.

If that describes you, don't let deciding how to live the rest of your life be one of the things that never gets decided. After reading this book you may decide that living in a 55+ community is not what you want to do, but at least you bought this book and looked into it. You made a decision.

One final thought about living in two different places is that the two places you live could be in a 55+ park part of the year and in a motorhome part of the year.

I know people who have chosen that lifestyle and thoroughly enjoy it.

You Can Afford It

Previously I talked about comparing the upfront cost and living expenses of living in a 55+ park with living in a motorhome. I used the example of a $35,000 home and a $35,000 motorhome.

Keep in mind that you can get some very nice motorhomes in the $15,000 to $20,000 range and, of course, you can get homes in 55+ communities in that range as well. A $20,000 home and a $15,000 RV would still give you the same $35,000 total investment.

Having the option to live your retirement in a fun and enjoyable way is what you've worked for all your life.

Of course, staying where you are and not changing anything is an option and it has its advantages. If that's what you end up doing, let it be because that's what you decided to do and not because you just never got around to making a decision about what you wanted to do.

Chapter 14

Summary

For the first time in a long time – maybe for the first time ever – you may be finding yourself in a situation where you have complete freedom to do whatever it is you want to do and live wherever you want to live.

Obviously, one of the options you are considering is moving into a 55+ park, otherwise you wouldn't have purchased this book.

The purpose of this book is not to convince you to move into a 55+ community or to choose any of the other lifestyle options described in the book.

The purpose of the book is to give you inside information about what the 55+ lifestyle is about and some idea about what it will cost along with some pros and cons.

And, as you've noticed, I've included information on three other lifestyles that you might not have thought about.

It's great to now have the freedom to make a decision based almost entirely on what you would like to do and where you would enjoy living. Almost all of your life, where you have lived has been dictated to a large extent by jobs, schools, families and, let's face it, just plain habit.

Now is your chance, while you are still able to enjoy life, to make a decision with the main criteria being where will you be the happiest and be able to enjoy life the most?

The good part is that the lifestyles that may give you the most enjoyment won't cost an arm and a leg. With one or two Social Security checks a month, maybe a small pension check, maybe a few savings (or equity in a home that you could sell) and maybe earning a little bit of money each month doing something you really enjoy, you can live the lifestyles described in this book. You don't have to have all of the possible income sources described above to make it work.

A lot of financial advisers will do some calculations and show you how many millions you will need to retire, but this is based on continuing to live the expensive life you are living now—with a big house and big expenses.

Reverse the way you look at your retirement. Instead of figuring out how much money you will need to retire, figure out how much money you will have coming in and look at what kind of lifestyle you can have on that income.

You may find that scaling your expenses and obligations back and living a totally different lifestyle might bring you a lot more enjoyment and a lot less stress.

At least it deserves some thought. Obviously, you're giving it some thought because you're reading this book. Take these facts, observations and inside information from someone who has 'been there and done that' and picture yourself in a different lifestyle versus your present lifestyle and think about which way you would be happier.

It's easier not to make a decision and just do what you've always done, but if you end up not changing your lifestyle, let it be because you considered all of the options and came to the conclusions that living your present lifestyle is what would make you the happiest. Don't let it be because you just never got around to making a decision.

And, who knows, I may soon see you in a 55+ park—in fact, I might even be your neighbor. I'm 72 and I don't plan on driving this motorhome around forever. On second thought, I have an uncle who is 92 and he is still driving his motorhome. His is four feet longer than mine. He lives in Charleston, South Carolina, and has recently driven his RV to Pennsylvania and to Florida. He likes to go. I think I will be in a 55+ park way before I get to be 92.

Just because you're getting older doesn't mean that you can't be active and do fun things. I didn't run my first marathon until after I turned 60.

I hope to see you in a 55+ park soon.

If you have questions for me, feel free to email me at Jminchey@gmail.com.

About the Author

Jerry Minchey is the author of several books. He has a bachelor's degree in electrical engineering, an MBA from USC, and an OPM degree from Harvard Business School. He worked for NASA on the Apollo moon mission and worked for many years as a computer design engineer.

He has owned several engineering and marketing businesses. Now semi-retired, he is the founder and editor of two Internet subscription websites – MarketingYourRestaurant.com and SearchEngineU.com.

As an engineer and a business major, he looks at problems from both a logical standpoint as well as an economic and financial standpoint.

That's the approach he takes when analyzing the pros and cons of moving into a 55+ community. He also draws from his first hand experience of living in 55+ parks. His parents owned and lived in 55+ parks for 15 years, buying and selling homes along the way.

With numerous uncles, aunts, cousins and friends retiring and moving into 55+ parks over the years, he had a world of knowledge and experience to draw on when he set out to research and report on the advantages of moving into a 55+ park.

He presently lives full-time in his motorhome and travels between the North Carolina mountains in the summers and the Florida beaches in the winters— plus several side trips throughout the year. He says, "Home is wherever I park it."

Index

CPSIA information can be obtained
at www.ICGtesting.com
Printed in the USA
LVHW081140041120
670677LV00040B/658

9 780984 496822